THE GOLDEN PILGRIMAGE

THE GOLDEN PILGRIMAGE

୶

99 *Sonnets* by

STEVEN NIGHTINGALE

RAINSHADOW EDITIONS
THE BLACK ROCK PRESS
2011

Cloth Edition:
ISBN: 978-1-891033-55-1

Trade Paper Edition:

ISBN: 978-1-891033-56-8

Library of Congress Control Number: 2011939182

The Black Rock Press
University of Nevada, Reno Reno, NV 89557-0244
www.blackrockpress.org
Printed in the United States of America

Cover Image:
Mohammed (c.570-c.632) and the Archangel Gabriel, from
the 'Siyer-i Nebi' (gouache on paper) by Turkish School (16th
century) Topkapi Palace Museum, Istanbul, Turkey/ Bildarchiv
Steffens/ The Bridgeman Art Library

For Lucia and Gabriella
—mi música, mi aventura, mi luz

Contents

Introduction

SOME POEMS, STORIES, AND NOVELS of the present and of past centuries are infused with harmony and clarity, with orchestral energy; they hold such a beckoning and a consummation in beauty, that they remake our minds and manner of life. Our study of them builds around us a house where we can live, and frees the mind so that it may carry on with a fateful journey. We might call it our golden pilgrimage.

Yet the principles and meaning of such work are called often into question by current opinion and culture, with its melancholy and suspicion. The idea that beauty calls us to clarity and life is mocked. A sense that the earth offers us with grace and gift-giving labors a power, a provenance, a destination—this is seen as fanciful. The notion of peace as a living reality, a quality of mind and work, is treated as sentiment—trivial when compared to the melodrama of conflict and grandeur of emotion. The soul, conceived as that part of the body which may be made permanent by love, is now scorned, or swollen and infected by religious pride.

Neither the sonnet, as a form, nor this writer, as a man, can deny literary stakeholders or the historical moment. But to submit to such influence is another matter, bound up with conscience and experience. And as conscience is fierce and searching, so experience is delicious and determinative. With these resources we may resist a coarse commercial chant, the hymn of contempt in fundamentalist belief, the noisy glamour of violence in books and politics, and the booming invitations to waste and obedience that blow through our daily lives.

We live in this pandemonium, but off to the side, nearby, without fanfare, in a quiet hour, even in the tempest of the news, you will hear if you seek to hear a trustworthy whisper, an amorous overture, a movement of wings, a small song: the *sonetto*, our sonnet. For more than eight hundred years this form has been used to sing to us of our chance to travel where peace flourishes, where beauty offers irresistible life, where the soul has at last a savor of home.

A small song, yet in just the way love might have a small beginning—a bemused glance across a room, an unexpected grace note in conversation, a sudden embrace in the twilight.

These sonnets now are yours. They are your companions. I write them because of your blessed travels toward life. If you find them familiar, there is a reason. You are the reason—the way you love, the world you make, the beauty you give.

—S. N.
North Yuba Canyon, July 2010

Sonnets about You

What if in fourteen lines, is infinite
Space and all history, coyote's wit,

Holy candlelight, musk of your lover
In the tropics? What if a right metaphor
Is the house of peace? If a woolen cover

Of plain celestial thread may be knit
By a mother, tucked musically by her
Around a baby, and history has a cure
Because of the two of them? What if

Inside a sonnet, is nutmeg, jokes, a voyage
With children among myriad stars; a door
Where you walk from yourself to a lineage

Of souls, who speak to us of light, of duty—
By your work, reader, we will dwell in beauty.

She Begins the Only Work

You can say it: it's time to begin
World again, as you arise to begin

Yourself again. In stories of children,
It's pixie dust or a magic wand, illustrative
Of powers that crisscross in light, run

Through midmost of bones: our force
In thunderstorms, river rapids, soft rain,
Movement of python or puma. The pain
Will be unspeakable. The privilege, a divorce

From habit, misery, old canny ignorance
And comprehensive hatred. You will give
Away original treasure. It is a sundance

Beyond your death. Around the river's bend,
Inside a jewel, with a song: it's time to begin.

About That Body of Yours

What if the body likes having a soul?
If flesh is what you need to be whole?

So that, in love, you understood how
You are a visitor, your gift this place
To sing. Years pass, you learn how

You are made of grass, honeycomb, big
Storms blowing off cobalt oceans, salsa
Bands in tropical bars, roses, balsa
Wood and sandstone, the succulent fig,

Granite, wild blackberries: you are made
Of earth because you are made of grace,
Both sandpiper and planet: you are made

For this peace, for learned delectation.
Soul chooses flesh. Skin is revelation.

And You Thought It Was Disorganized—

What if it's all of a piece? If you
Still need to do dishes, review

The accounts, yet go on that evening
To roughhouse with the heavens, confer
With falling stars who in a forest clearing

Muse with you on a design for the day
Just on the way, as with their light
You stitch together the hours. The right
You have, you earned, which is to play

In just this labor, loving the thread
Of life, tying body to soul by signature.
Having undone darkness, you are led

Back to your house, the dishes, the lease,
The pencil, the godhead, it's all of a piece.

Abdal

Then one day his life stopped. He
Changed, as, say, plain rock you see

In space, changes into a ready planet
With oceans, numbers, cougars, wonders,
Jokes, ice cream, hope. He set

His life on a crooked course, that,
Though few understood, held within
A trust and blaze of light. From cat
To heaven, all of life—dream and reason

And genius of mint breeze in summer
Passing over lovers—all of life hungers
To have just this change: the thunder

In the heart, the lightning in the mind,
Soul at home, annunciation by design.

For You, At Work in the Garden

Everyday is a seed-bed, and its flowers
Are formed by earth and trusted powers,

Since flowers, when they are perfect,
Disappear into what they mean. Just
As when the world, lovely and bereft,

Disappears into you and me. So flowers
Are everywhere, and so could we love
A chance on earth, time true and rough,
With calloused hands tending the hours

We have. We know, as we work, how
World is not given as paradise, but
Raw material of paradise; and how

We may garden here, with love's help.
Garden until the earth turns into itself.

Thet Thar World In Ya

Fever and fraud, pain, chaos, sin,
Yet you can make a world within

That has a final starlight and legend.
It has the sound of a flute in the forest,
Movement of blue whales who ascend

Through centuries; it has hummingbirds
Drilling gushers of color in air, herds
Of antelope with hymns in their blood,
Drops of water on a honeysuckle bud,

The anaconda coiled around her eggs;
It has a woman doing cartwheels to bless
The desert light; it has the kitchen rags

Loved to shreds. It has what we are given:
Cinnamon, dirt, song, ordinary heaven.

Time, Let's Take It On

Time is not transparent killing. It
Is just the way our mind works. It

Is hunger's scapegoat, has no violence
But our violence. Beyond all the misery
Time shows beauty of riotous innocence.

Time stops, but for peace only. Only
For peace. Where are we then, when
In that place, after such loving, instead
Of passage of hours, now there is only

Singing, arcane, smoky circus lights?
When in us is decorum of melody
As of herons soaring together, your nights

Earthly learned fireworks? Come true
Outside of time; O how liberty becomes you—

Everything That Is, Is More

It is not a book, not a tempest, not
A honeycomb or handful of rain; not

Just dance steps holding a cadence
Of sentences you hope to whisper
To a lover next summer. The defense

Of the world, is that it is just not
The world, you are not yourself,
A word not merely word. A thought
May like a calico cat on a shelf

Leap onto the earth, taking a library
With her. Your traveling hope will stir
Trees like wind. You'll pick a blackberry

As a gift for a child of storytelling eyes,
Who labors for the nectary of sunrise.

That Old and New Door

In the air, wherever you are, a door,
Built over millenniums. In the solar core

Of yourself, powers, simplicity of fate,
A key. That bemused rapturous beauty,
Is it our introductory planet? Do you wake

A constellation of familiar stars in you,
Walk into a forest to talk with wolves?
The flare of song finds you, and curves
Away to surety, trust, a sensuality true

And mindful, and shows you the door
In the air, wherever you are. Your duty
Is beautiful work: vanishing. Fairest shore

Of adventure, is in yourself. Before you,
The nova, a laughter: what you must do.

You Were Worried About Salvation

Would you be doomed, because there is
More joy than there is time; there is

More music than notes and keys,
More beauties than numbers, more
Clarity, messages, coolness in a breeze

Off the sea, than in all heavens together?
Would you be saved when a blade of grass
Arcs into the next world; the ebullient cast
Of a play has prophecy and quick measure

Of history; a painting on a wall summons
A sapphire galaxy close; an everyday chore
Leads you to analects of light; the seasons

Are juggled in a lover's hands, and you learn,
You stand forth and love the light you earn—

What?

As wings are, as light is, so
Flesh may be; as you know,

Then you live, when your thought
Is more than a pinned butterfly or
A polished set of weathervanes caught

In a storm-siege of history; more than
Leaves of a tree in autumn, now longing
Only for decomposition. Your belonging
To creation, means the soil knows when

You can be trusted. Mountains are made
By phrases. A swirling rocky shore
Rowdy with seaweed and loons, is made

By hand. World is mind when true.
What is waiting to be made by you?

Stanzas Made Material

The alembic of language, over your fire—
Watch how the world changes: a lyre

Shows along a whole wild coast, in lines
Of waves played by wind; and shows in
A band of feathers, hawk's wing designed

Over millennia with rapture by a genius
In radiant air; shows in the raw layers
Of rock in the wall of a canyon, a trust
Composed for us, music of two players—

Water and stone. To alembic of language
Comes life only by a simmering within
You, your combustible adventure. The adage

You find in an old book on a cold day
Will safeguard every girl, as you pray.

Invisible World Having a Lark

When it moves we call it wind,
Calling of cosmos upon our skin,

From homeground of grace. Who
Is this come to heal, to ask you if
You will learn transfiguration? Do

You know how to fly? Can you
Disappear? What is this wild music
Everywhere in air, hobo kazoo?
Will you see through the change, trick,

Sleight of world? See acrobatic proof
Of generosity irresistible? Through riff
And planetary concerto, only one proof:

Invisibility. It comes, we call it wind—
Bemused interstellar movement within.

You're Ordinary,
but There's Upside in This Deal

And if a candor of light is meant to
Live in you? If the still center, cool

And perfect, of a cyclone, is meant to
Be your mind in the buffets of history?
A nonchalance of flamingoes meant to

Show the curious, playful way you
Put together phrases? Since world
Envelops you, centerpoint of world
Is everywhere, what you once knew

And can know calls you in this place
Where you are sent so heaven can see
Just what you will do with this grace—

A lovely hunger of earth. Be consumed
By ordinary sunlight in an ordinary room.

The Fitness of Things

Words fit with what they mean, as do
Leaf and light, wind and whitecap, blue

Of a tropic sea and musical eyes of a lover
In the morning; they fit, as do cyclones
To the motion of mind, or a quilt cover

On a cherished sleeping child. Our words
Fit within the world, as a song matches
Steps in dance, a cloak of colored patches
Is guide to events and destiny, the turns

Of two dancers in love in a country bar
Trace out the play of light that combs
Beauty across the river; as a star

At dawn fits into the palm of a hand,
When love is first gift and last stand.

One of Her Simple Days and Nights

A geyser coming up in the front yard;
In your hands, every day, the wild card

Of your fate. You are meant to play
At the table of earth and this heaven,
No other place—this place, this day,

With your life, in your flesh, with no
Hopes but those written on your soul
At the beginning. Was that you, the fool
Walking at dawn into the clown-show

Of beauty, by that line-dance of ocean
Along the coast, symposium of fog? Seven
Colors of a rainbow at midnight, they bend

To you and your lover, arc of your pleasure.
Bring us the future. It is female treasure.

Not Easy, But Maybe It's Worth It

At miracle-working, motley crossroads of love,
A world waits, goblins give you a shove,
Roughnecks among angels tease and fight,
Bruise you with visions, teach what the night

Knows: thrones are useless—thrones of kings,
Words, wealth, reason, dreams, yourself.
Beyond talk and bills, paychecks and key rings,
And death, shrunken head on a kitchen shelf,

There is movement and a movement, there
Is movement in the middle of this world. Now
You have the answer, since worlds endow
Only the treasure you can hold, when you dare

Travel with friends, angels roughhouse above,
At miracle-working, motley crossroads of love.

The Future of Conversation

What if a man is made of song? If song
Were entrusted to him, as lights belong

To a ruby, as grace belongs to cranes
In the love-dance of spring; as beauty
Belongs to a wild river. The refrains

Of such music remake, in trust, by gift,
The air and us. So a heaven may begin
Here and again, to search, then to season
Mind and body, soul and word; and lift

All world. Must we come apart in a strut,
Excitement and puffery of discord—greedy
To have the money of emotion? In the gut

Of history, we are stuffed, victorious, sick—
Until we make our talk a truthful music.

Workaday Invitation of Sagebrush

In soft sidelit rain of the high desert
I met a spirit. All I had learnt

Was strange prelude to what she said.
First, that each small gray-green leaf
Of every sage, each day, is homestead—

Is invitation. Paradise is not promise,
But workaday offering: the well where
We find our laughter, then the stair
We climb to talk with stars, the trick

We need to dream away temporary lives
And take form anew. She said the relief
From agony is certain, that death thrives

In the world, only to heal. Just to heal.
The cosmos you own, you must unseal.

One-Liners

You have what you give. How you love
Configures a soul. Every world above

Is below and within. Mind and heart
Conjure one another. Wind off the sea
Moves the grasses to signal the lark

Who sings to the moon. You can vanish
With the banner of any beauty. History
Hopes only to belong to you. The story
Held in a hummingbird's eye will banish

Rancor everywhere. In you, snake's coil
And winged noon light. You will be free
When old rampant turmoil, the boil

Of personality, is set aside. In the sod
You will be a worm and will be a god.

One-Liners II

The light is conscious. The north wind
Will carry your mind away, and upend

Crude history with planetary adventure.
Your lover will bring to your bed tonight
Whitewater, a mountainside of flowers, tour

Of cinnamon, sweat, and jam, and then
In darkness cherish the moment when
Summer comes forth in you. You can send
For winter, say you are ready, and tend

Snowflakes come for consultation. Earth
Needs your profile and songline. What is right
Is known to thunder and granite. The church

Will rise within the story that you are,
When work in you is an opalescent star.

One-Liners III

History has given you a gift on trust.
Eagle chicks visit you. You make dust

Into water, into gold, into whatever
Form of mind, because the world is
What we understand, now, forever—

Pattern-book of what we understand.
By this law, you are the one who must
Signal springtime to begin, when crust
Of failure and habit breaks, all the land

Is before us, within us, and your music
Is our justice and honey; when your wit
Is outlandish sacrament; when the trick

And glory, tryst and fireworks of spring
Is your offering from life on the wing.

One-Liners IV

Your blood is all of song and starlight.
World is canvas painted by your sight.

When you die, become what you know.
You'll run with coyotes, fly with a crow.
You may be mist, river, ocean, snow.

All this, because one day you knew that
As a ragtag visitor you can laugh, since
Every minute is a joke from heaven, since
Every minute is jeweled with trust that

You will find a way into the summertime
Of understanding. What you will bestow
On life, is the book about how to shine

With hours made of plain cosmic dalliance.
The amorous is factual, mindful radiance.

The Joinery of Things

A tear, and first spring rain; the breath
That begins the hurricane. The one death

That leads on to holocaust; sincere nod
Of a calm man that means dismemberment
By machete of thousands. Manufactured god

That generations use to carry through
With acrimony of detail, pride and awe,
A sordid campaign that will forever undo
Dreams of ten million girls. One slipshod

Calculation melts a city. One small kindness
Will sweeten a millennium. One letter sent
Means understanding, long peace, a caress

From history. Cosmos is given from hand
To hand. When will you make your stand?

The Sorrow of Her

After such energy, I would not have thought
That a language of sunlight that you sought,

Orchestral commentary of starlight, dance
Of years and words changing places under
A new moon; or painting known in a trance

As though flowers, mountains, animals,
Dipped the brushes of what they can give
Into the history of beauty—after such spells
So clear, after such suffering, as you live,

I would not have thought that your weather
Of heart had lost the iridescent thunder
Of your hope, nor that the burning leather

That ties you to yourself, by thoughts,
Had so many proud demonic knots.

What! We're Supposed to Go Somewhere?

What you see and do, neglect and revere,
The hot tar of misfortune, alcoholic cheer,

Your dressage of honors, noble conviction
Of family, everything you hope and fear:
All this is the anchor, rusted dereliction

Holding you in a thick mud of society.
Yet you know: being afloat is being alive.
You worship wind, clear raucous deity.
Occasionally, to cheers, you strip and dive

Down into the slop, to slowly rise
With hallelujahs, break out kegs of beer,
And be a good fellow. You forget the cries

Of blessed gulls, turquoise glittering details—
Forget the beautiful boat, the rope and sails.

You Think You Are No One?

My friend, my dear friend, you live as if
Nothing is lost, no one rots within. As if

Casual neglect on a hot afternoon—a call
Not made, letter not composed, a confidence
Brushed off; as if the well-reasoned fall

Into lazy irritation or miniscule hatred—
As if you pretend you don't know
What it means: a young woman dead,
Her green eyes pecked out by a crow;

A machete in the neck of a child who
Was weary of backhanded slaps; a cadence
Of lovely guns—the bullets make stew

Of your country: you think you are no one?
We are careless, stylish, and cancel the sun.

Dinner Party

Easy conversation: because our minds are
Frozen, we have this crude skating. We are

Moving into the rancor of cold, as we die
At the table. We have been well-nourished
And know how to slaughter. We are shy,

Then coiled in disquiet, then content;
Finally we are joyful, relieved to be dead
One more night. Everything we meant
Will fit like a noose on each pretty neck.

A trapdoor falls after dessert, and no one
Notices: that's the glory. We have flourished
Here. It's bestial, but with good nutrition.

Our education led us to health and liberty.
Dead souls, but learned, comforted, free.

The Problem of the Obvious

I'm sorry to point out the ax in your forehead,
Napalm in the mailbox, pit viper in your bed.

Excuse me, your funeral has been scheduled
For next Thursday, and that brain tumor
Will burst today. A pity you've been fooled—

Tomorrow, when you turn the handle, no water
Will run from the tap, and yes, that's a volcano
Coming out of the lawn. In the tropics, snow.
Oceans seethe with acid, and the slaughter

Of the innocents is daily, without comment.
You should note the horned demon at the door,
The tidal waves turning to fire, the recent

Note in the mail, about the curious bacteria
Making soup of flesh, by apocalyptic criteria.

At the Computer,
regretting the Billion Dead

At least it's efficient now, the famine. We
Can watch each other die on a screen, we

Stream video from the inferno, which
Is just such a pity. Yet we ask, being
Reflective: is it avant-garde? Is it kitsch,

This wave of extermination? Or just destiny,
With a classical savor? It's true, we were told
Catastrophe was nearby, winking inside history,
And waiting until we were ebullient in gold,

Education, and costume parties. Then, suddenly
Everything was ready. Absurd angel wings,
An apocalypse without a god, death comely

After this suffering. Rise, we are not defeated!
You will be selected, and you will be deleted.

Evil Is Always Like This

It's not that they were vicious, that
Flesh-eating spit filled them, that

Lurid in faces we saw a blast furnace
Of hatred. No such thing. It was that
They were calm and sent men to brush

Poison on the eyes of children. They were
Reasonable and weary, when giving the order
To crush a hundred cities, giving the order
For technicolor crescendo of death. They were

Resigned, knowing, regretful men. They
Came from nice families, all with a knack
For power, loyalty, tradition. Every day

Has its cabernet and holocaust. Every day
The dignified pestilence of what they say.

Salvation by Crow

I have not known sorrow, unless you mean
The tears like poisoned claws that clean

Flesh from my face; or the nausea before
Any mirror, as body darkens to show
A bucket of guts, blue flies in a swarm—

Full joyful trance of appetite; or knowing
Any broken blade of grass has a soul
Of beauty beyond any labor of mine. A whole
Life wasted, guttural death daily uncoiling

In phrases and failures. I have not known
Sorrow, except the sledgehammer's blow
In the face as I leave the house, the roam

Of maggots in the bone marrow, as I go
To pray I will be eaten today by a crow.

Did You Say Despair?

You mean when my thoughts are like shrapnel,
Cutting tissue all day, hollowing me for hell,

Who swarms on the street and in the house,
Liquid garbage alive; you mean television
Like a mortar attack, come to announce

Sequined hysterical degradation? Is that it?
Do you mean a generation learning to kill
For a spot in the garbage dump, slow thrill
Of roasting the neighbors alive, a clean hit

With an ax to split the head of history?
Am I mistaken? Do you mean permission
From a fat demon to enter the sacristy

Of headquarters, where with swagger and beauty
We proclaim extermination as our holy duty?

Self-Made Man Sees What Self Makes

Face it, my friend: inside your brain
A bomb is ticking, A fragrant spring rain

Will make no difference. The lioness
Rowdy in morning sun, mustang in a canyon
Beloved and glistening, are sudden death

To you, because of the cave-in that is
The way you have lived. Wildflowers
Will not save you. No one will miss
You, your idolatry of human powers,

Bauble of renown. In the worlds, nothing
But gifts incalculable, celebration among
A coloratura of beauties. You are gutting

Heaven, music, story, soul's wealth.
Hell does not exist. It is yourself.

Report on Niceness from the Next World

So nice. When I was sick, he even
Came to visit: best wishes, reason,

Empathy, a meal. Later, when food
Was scarce, imagine my surprise when,
Expensive gun in hand, in a good mood,

He shot a plump young man on the street,
Gutted him with finesse, dragged him home
Behind his car, and cut out a thigh bone
To suck the marrow, as waves of heat

Rose from the burning city. I was sick
Again, because I knew I could depend
On him. He came to the door, with a kick

Shattered the wood, the lock, my mind. By
A sadism of courtesy, I took a month to die.

Coming Soon to a Nation Like Yours

They will be lucky, the ones eaten raw
By their neighbors. There is no law

Saying that only so many can die.
Families herded like pigs, to a sty
And shot all at once, hung high,

Hosed down, gutted for good meat,
Put in military freezers. Hoarse men
With guns move fashionably to defend
A glamour of hatred, virile sugar, sweet

Hot legend. Rich whores use recipes
For fresh brains of children, they fry
Them for friends. Inspirational screams

Are holy music. The future, take a look:
A mother flayed alive, for reading a book.

Against All Advice, She Divorces Him

I say goodbye to him, whom I leave
Forever, though time had me cleave

To him, though everyone had told me
My body had his name, they had told me
I promised unto death, they had told me,

They had told me, their phrases winding
Like a python to amicably crush me,
Digest me in friendship. Such reminding
Now is called faith. To a muscular dream

Of devotion I leave them, their lifetime
Of glory and judgment. Goodbye. I can see
Your saccharine hatred. I seek the design

Of a key that fits the lock of my years.
A door swings open, to shatter the mirrors.

If I May Share My Madness

A stampede of language. I had no mind—
It had me. I could not hold a glass of wine

Since resurgent within it was a vineyard,
The weather there and a woman who touched
The grapes, the way she tastes, and a shard

Of pottery from another century in the soil.
I left the table, staggered outside, and saw
Tiny wildflowers talking with the moon, saw
Stars take form on earth as children, a roil

And waterfall of children, dark in secrets, though
Still in their eyes starlight gleamed. They roughed
Up history and would save us, as a white crow

Flew from the zenith to a sky that opened
Inside my words. I am whole when broken.

A Soul From Beyond the Stars

Finally, a prison break, your constancy
Of inaugural light, a grace and fidelity

In you ascending, as delicious unities
Take you over. By bolt of conscience we
Recognize life in you. The entreaties

Of starlight in deep space, we feel now
In every cell, in every step, because
Of a riptide of love on earth, because
With you we work. By a brilliant plow

Of years drawn over all our faces,
We see what time does and why. We
Will know one another, all our faces

Irradiated finally by soul, all sorrow
Gone into the detonation of tomorrow.

Near Inverness

Beyond this misery, before this misery, I
See resurgent starlight and wild rivers. I

See a marsh whose movement has more birds
Than water, more sky than birds, more water
Than light, more light than heaven. Words

Fit there, in the shimmering; float there
In finesse, in clarity, a force-field of life.
Beyond this hatred, before this hatred, I
See how the sunlight, conscious and fair,

Singsong, amorous, curious, young, true,
Comes to care for you, son or daughter,
Solitary or singing to us. Whatever you do,

You were born into this musical peace,
Commonwealth, safety, winged release.

Living by the River

More than light: a sweetness within light.
More than darkness: traveling we incite

When we love with stories. More than
A river, but all an emerald delectation,
Water as logic, music of a string band

With notes of granite and cedar; harmony
Made of earth but answered by a heaven
We hear finally in a song that is leaven
Of memory, long musing sacred joinery,

The current in us: headwater, ocean,
Glossy acrobatic bend and riff of creation,
Wheeling color, surety, song; commotion

That is making souls. In whitewater rush
A perfect disheveled peace delivered to us.

Coming to the Cabin at Night

Stars whirling, ignited, as though held
High, a candelabra borne by an angel

In casual otherworldly helpfulness; the river
Humming, rambunctious, songstruck, wild
With learned storytelling tricks, our cure,

Hymn continuous, plan and praise, sound
That is the spinning of earth. Every stone
Loves this wild current: our mind, a home.
We who were lost, in life now are found.

This is music of what we love, unbound
In a canyon of the last secret, where time
Has surrendered every power to renown

Of melodic water and savor of blackberry—
Where life and death whisper and marry.

A Note On War

I know the big drum of hatred booms
In your head; in spit-polished rooms

With infernal silken colleagues, you throw
A switch and a school explodes. But we
Will defeat you. Every star and crow

Is on our side, and canyons, the river,
Coyotes, advent of sunrise on a coastline
Whose waves, each one, muse and deliver
A sentence in a long poem that we sign

Because of life. Because of earth. We
Have a military: the grass. Every blade we
Count as a soldier; every mountain, tree

And stone our accomplice, our beloved, friend—
With thermonuclear beauty we'll fight to the end.

And You Thought Paradise Was Dull

Undone by violence of paradise, he went
To the mirror, saw no one; but the present

And future played like cats, clouds improvised
With light, dreams and morning joined hands.
He did not notice his own absence, as cries

Of brilliant seabirds split the darkness
In history, forever. Hatred was pulled from
All of us like rotten teeth, the stupid drum
Of war pawned for a tambourine, the press

Of fatuous news waved aside like
Pestilent vapors; weekend country bands
Were bemused luminosity in fearful night

Of infernal confusions: we walk forth, forgive—
Love is heaven's rage, and it's time to live.

The Student of Hours

I loved you because you thought that
All was not lost. You alone. The rat

Of ambition ate happily into the brains
Of your brilliant friends. They wanted
To think something, the losses and gains

Lovingly calculated, gilt career conceived.
You wanted to do something. The sunlight
And concerto of your desert took flight
Within you. If arroyo and cactus achieved

Song and transcendence daily, why not all
Of us? Our vainglorious country, vaunted
University—yet the homely infinite call

Everyone can hear, if they would listen—
You wanted light. They wanted to glisten.

A Beloved Woman Goes Traveling

A beauty is permanent, if you make
It so. All world is here for the sake

Of heaven, is here for your hands—
For a touch of such slow love, it takes
A whole life. May you find heartlands

Inside what you see, what you know.
Hour by hour, may you trust, ascend,
Compose the wilderness you are; show
A phrase that catches light like aspen—

Or like the desert lake we love. You will
Do that, or something better. What makes
Our desert perfect, has changed you. Till

Those home grounds of soul, sow the seed.
You are meant for just the heaven you need.

Something About Her

Because she was a visitor, one of us,
She loved her adopted home. Her dust,

The clay that composes us, she formed
By choice around a form infinite,
Amused, perfect, explosive, charmed:

Not shape, but the source of shape; not
Time, but the old comedy in time; not
Earth, but its origin in beauty; not
Love, but its traveling in light; not

Herself, but anyone she wants to be.
She flies with falcons, trades in wit.
Would we learn, and live in liberty?

She is your friend; go then to her.
Personality is sickness; life, cure.

The Sight of You

As though you were a wild fair sapling
About to burst into flower, decanting

Song, softness, a musk and comeliness
Of adventures in love, your body molded
Of lickerish beatific energies, at behest

Of music in you; as though a river at noon,
All cutloose freelance phosphor, your light
At liberty beyond the suffering dark fight
Of daily world. A heron flies to the moon.

By female radiance, you show grace
As carnal mischief, languorously folded
In walk and glance, so that I taste

You when I touch you; as though you
Were the liquor of life: amorous brew.

The Strange Gold of Her Days

Then the call, like a thunderclap in a cloud
Full of music; a star-bound redwood bowed

Down to a snake, an emerald river changed
Course and ran through her hands, coyotes
Took her notebooks in their teeth and ranged

Inside her phrases. In a plain glass she
Holds, the water freezes, or boils; a colt,
Glossy and speaking, is born from a bolt
Of lightning one morning. What we need

Is what we learn from her, and from crows
In bemused dark carnival, or silent peyote
Dense with legends. What the world knows

She helps to make, from bedraggled soul.
She drinks life from beauty's golden bowl.

The Book of Eyes

A mint green eye: the reef shark.
Eye to hold a desert: meadowlark.

Eyes like coin of heaven: coyote.
Eyes tracking fool and devil: crow.
Eyes begun in green flesh: peyote.

Eyes that mark the light: a teacher.
Eyes like sheet-lightning: the owl.
Eyes of revelation: puma on the prowl.
Eyes like ovens: wealthy preacher.

Eyes of beatific tornadoes: a child.
Eyes of the coward: flakes of snow.
Eyes of whole current in rivers wild

By morning light, blood-song dreamt of,
And all new moons: this woman in love.

Another Prophet Living on Your Block

They looked for heaven in the sky.
She found it in any cartoon, and I

Followed her secretly, to watch as she
Winked, to summon mountain ranges
Of the next millennium; then as she

Showed paradise in a pebble. Rancor
Made her laugh. Sadness led her
To dress in revelation. She was commodore
Of deserts and formal dinners. The purr

Of moving hands in the raucous midmost
Of her night—the perfect whirling changes,
Fleshly spiritous female adventure; her coast

To morning on hot soft bright winds—
Every hour, her life begins and ends.

The World Is Fallen. In Love, For Instance.

Because one place marries another: a cove
In Maine visits a volcano in Java, a loaf

Of bread in a bakery in Rome is eaten
Fresh in a café in Tahiti. You embrace
A woman in Berlin, the two of you sweeten

A bed in the morning in a cabin high
In a canyon in the redrock country. Places
Move in you like rivers, offering graces
And carrying away your prayers. The cry

Of a macaw in the rain forest amuses
A baby born on pack ice; the lace
In a window in Paris, a young girl uses

As a map, a pattern, sign and clue,
Across the worlds she will visit you.

Truth Again, That Wild Pesky Thing

It is the color of sweetness, sound of justice.
A friendly comet, doorway in coastal mist;

Method of a hurricane, music inside granite;
Business of the rainbow, book written by
A baby asleep; it is ice cream and sonnet,

Singsong and zephyr, galaxy and toy,
A solar flare that licks your forehead,
Swatting away death. It is ordinary bread
Made of heaven and moonlight; a joy

In candor of plain fact, that makes
Life, life, life, and life only.
Truth is a woman. Eating mandrakes,

She showed how we are here for revelation—
How world would be you, reader: in creation.

Highly Sexed Young Woman Ordained

She spoke to us for her clear minute.
She had news. Just as a single shoot

Of grass is also sunlight and air; as
A puma is liquor of grace; as a planet
Makes beauty with morning and children, as

Hummingbirds in secret visit the dark side
Of the moon—just so: the Incarnation
Did not happen once. It is soul-delectation.
Simple fact. A traveling of young stars

To rebuke darkness. Not mere doctrine, but idea
At centermost of mind, your mind, if you reject
History's myriad contemptuous appetites: the idea

Is your flesh, your future, your eyes, your soul—
Work and joke: world divine, and you, whole.

A Couple in Wild Country

Lovers shotgunned with delectation, then
In dawn light walking hand in hand, when

A hawk came to their call, bull snakes
Offered them a proof of beauty, owls
Spoke with the buckskin sunset, lakes

Played like kittens with the crescent moon.
They once more in their devotions found
A way to move so they were unbound
In musk and honey on the high mesa. Soon

In fragrant starlight, young wild horses
Will move like blessing through sage, howls
Of a coyote assemble songs and forces

Of full peace. Bolt of lover's pleasure
Is dream-torrent of earth; dust, treasure—

Seven Times

What has been delicious, now I see
Was preparation for you, my beauty:

Seven times the sweetness of this earth,
Seven times the heaven hidden in stories,
Seven times a pleasure in body's church,

Seven times any true text, so that,
As I read in the sunlight a winged book,
Then I was flying, melodic winds shook
All sense, I burst at last from the trap

Of the world, so to return to beauties
With seven times life, all ordinary glories,
What were my rights now are my duties—

And seasons, river, all we sang of
Live now, live with seven times love.

Your Teaching and Your Loving

Long light on the river, a red-haired girl;
Snowflakes fall at midnight, a black pearl.
Desert mornings, my rising inside of you;
Oceans asleep and dreaming, all we do.

What is it, my beauty, that marries lovers,
And from fierce distance, brings riven life
Into a heaven of resemblance, and recovers
Love-making, the union, the form, the christ;

The motion that mothers us all, my beauty:
In your arms you make me, moving with you,
Whirlwinds of dreamwork turning us through
This world, toward another; a gift of fidelity

Good in every world. The morning is alive,
My sunlight, my mary, my witch, my bride.

A Man Cannot Believe His Good Luck

He laughed so hard his shadow changed color,
He drank so much the ground went stellar.

He had romance in his right hand, mischief
In his left: this was the day of his wedding.
This was marriage like dancing off a cliff—

Both of them winged. To their strange day
Every child in the world offered laughter.
They shone with trust. In the hereafter
They will have shy rendezvous; but today

She had mint and sugar on her lips, she
Led him a long way through their bedding.
Pleasure is a promise, a beauty, a key

To open the world of your one mate.
She is singsong flying delicious fate.

Luna de Miel

In the middle of the middle of the air,
Inside the inside of your amorous care,

Ordinary clairvoyance of day and night
That by what you do, in touch and hope,
Composes just this world: moving light

Within language, a countryside of olives,
Grapevines, sunflowers; your conversation
Of cinnamon and cream. Our morning lives,
Musical within you. All womanly creation

That I sought, you offer, at midmost
Of a midmost in loving, your grace note
Along rimrock and lost iridescent coast,

The musky intelligence of what you do—
A life within this life, inside of you.

What's Left of Them

Our bodies cast away, only a glimmer
Of sweat left. Clothes for the sinner,

But world for souls naked and undone
By lovemaking, first and flying gift
Given, all virtue, peach juice of reason

Given, raucous liturgy of long whispers
Given, oaths of allspice and final stars
Given, cream and memory and smoky bars
Given, music of rivers and of vespers

Chanted on mountains, skylarking trust
Given. What light comes to lift
Us into life, if not the austere, just,

Phosphorescence of generosity in bed—
Movement by wings, into the sacred?

Abundantly Naked

Nothing more tropical, then the smell
Of you abundantly naked, bud and shell

Of musky lips in candlelight, and you
Lost and found after hours of loving.
Nothing more beautiful: mind come true—

Religious sweat, regeneration of soul
When your body by threads of pleasure
Is spun again: formed from old measure
Of morning, mint, honeysuckle, fold

Of sugar and soil. Nothing more perfect
Than your lyrical fragrance. How loving
Becomes you, you are here to protect

The heaven you offer, the peace. I adore
A wise hot sheet-lightning in your languor.

Good Taste

She tasted like the tropics, I will not
Say how. When held down and caught

Up in hot sunlight and her long surf
Into her trustworthy pleasure, she gives
Forth a savor of warm grass and first

Mountain summer wildflowers, cinnamon,
Soil, nutmeg, allspice, cloves. I will
Not say I lived for these vapors, will
Not say how when she would come

I searched her nectary for such cream.
Devotion must go slow, and the sage
And salt of her second visitation mean

That any thing is possible here on earth—
One loved woman, is what life is worth.

What Is Possible

We trust the canyon rock. Fidelity
Holds peace beyond hope, a capacity

Within. Fragrant heat, flying meadow
And hot moist wind all move here
In the beginning of embraces: a slow

Season of sex, my beloved—may I earn
Beyond random lurid drumming fear,
A chance to stay in the world and learn
Landmarks of your rough beauty: dear

And dying like everyone, except for
A sure sensual aurora of soul, clear
As light off a wilderness coast, more

Than light, more than a river or aspen stand;
Love, I would stroke the shadow of your hand.

Just Words

Can word be water, word be earth?
Phrase be a flower, phrase be a perch

For a falcon? Can a sentence be
A crescent moon, good galaxy curled
With its armful of stars, tropical sea

Of enameled power come in peace?
For forgiveness they come. A paragraph,
My love, a stanza, a rhyme, with the yeast
Of your understanding, and a young seraph

In attendance, hungry herself, with heat
Of our hopes, will make bread. World
Is where language leads, love a street

Where I live for your song, your mouth—
Touch of your hand, stars of the south.

At Eleven Months

If I could summon a gilt spiral galaxy
To earth, or could touch brute anarchy

Into open peace, song, and patience;
If in a summer sweetgrass meadow set
In a candor of granite, I saw radiance

Of sleepy angels musing all morning;
If a mockingbird sang to me suggestions
Offered by a generosity of wings bearing
Wink and theology of wind; if questions

Flaming in me were answered by water
Falling clear in a canyon—if what met
Me here was all this, my little daughter,

It is nothing, next to your sleep of charms.
Nothing, next to the weight of you in my arms.

Parents Just Trying To See Straight

You learned to clap, sitting on the floor
Like a geyser of delight. A shining door

Made for you, in a movement of sunlight
Swung open. We could see what the earth
Was meant for. The hopes we had in sight

Long ago, now, rollicking daughter, you
Give into our understanding, loved one—
We take your hand, touch comes true.
We hold you, you teach us the reason

We must hold onto heaven. You are
The reason. May we come to be worth
Your touch, this luck, the reborn star

In your head that shows the first light,
Your mind in creation, planet set right.

Bad Dream

I will put your bad dream in a blast furnace,
Nothing will be left, not even ashes. The just

Hand of an angel will write out that dream,
Then read it aloud in a voice so sweet,
Fear will turn to sugar. Buck and stream

Of singing azure current, now of air,
Now of ocean, will bear your bad dream
Away forever, for evil can only seem,
Feign, taunt, threaten, bluster, dare—

But never be, little daughter. The message
Inside morning will undo your bad dream:
Peace cancels all damage, with heritage

Of another world. What is permanently true
Is the aurora of goodness inside of you.

Our Sleeping Wakeful Children

You sleep, arms flung over the pillow, as if
Flying among meadowlarks and novas, as if

The world can be trusted. Looking at you
I know it can be so. Yet the acid clamor,
Sneering, famine, massacre, daily school

Of beatings, humiliation, until our news
Is a tempest of poison—yet even this
Abomination will yield, the lethal drift
To catastrophe stop. Perfect raw blues

Dreamed by a mother on the dark street
Of a desperate city, can find and enamor
Our peace. We will learn, when we meet

Just these tough sacred children, who will go
To junk the ruinous gods, with what they know.

Granada in Her Unlikelihood

We found a field of stars, as we three
Walked together, one small family.

Even stone had ideas, changing color
According to a dialog with light—honey,
Then suede; now cognac, then stellar

Again, hopeful luscious glow of stars;
Finally, color of a gazelle, walls of rock
Lithe, ready to bolt into the sky. A clock
Here, keeps time of the mind. The bars

That lock in the songs of vision, fall
Away, everyone is offered the liberty
And secrets they can bear. After all,

We might live. You might live and thrive.
After such catastrophe, we are all alive.

Humdrum Cause and Effect

The crescent moon may be found hiding
In books at a flea market. Pull off siding

From the old barn, and you will uncover
A packet of seeds that you must take
To the desert to plant; the oil—pure,

Alive, delicious—taken from its leaves,
Will heal a soul, and that soul will heal
A century. The way a student conceives
Alone, at a small table of word and steel

In the basement of a big library, how to take
First steps on an opalescent road, to forsake
Her ideas of herself, to walk forth, to awake

From the trance of history—because of her,
We can learn how we are divinely impure.

On Laughter, Logic, and Salvation

The logic I love fits one atom to another,
And makes a whole Milky Way our brother,

Since galaxies and boys spin by trust
In the same laws; cobra and peacock
Depend on the same heart. A thin crust

Of green scum on a pond in the savannah,
Tomorrow, is an elephant, or an antelope,
Then a book, as our bright worlds float
In darkness to show the opalescent banner

That means life, when logic of matter
Has its source in logic of soul: a flock
Of scarlet ibis visits a baby to scatter

Beauty all through her. One day she
Will save us with the logic of comedy.

O the Perils of Loneliness

Once out of company, then you are
Visited: a tiger in the library, a star

Stopping by to ask directions, the island
You found in the attic, mentioned on all
The treasure maps of the world. You send

To a shy friend a note full of jokes,
Trust, and rubies. You sit by the fire
And read a book about thunder in a lyre,
About a woman whose sentence stokes

Justice in every heart, and bears a song
Into the territory of suffering. You call
Softly, and hear answer a beloved, strong,

From another century. The necessary food
For needful work is served only in solitude.

Anything Can Happen, Reader

Anything can happen. Yet what counts is
What happens within you, in you is

Old firestorm and tranquility of creation,
Both fury and dance, transcendental jokes,
Whirlpool, whippoorwill, singsong notation

By seagulls along the dream-drawn coast,
Bannered cities with secret houses whose
Basements are full of honey; in you, news
Of earth and death, mercy, the midmost

And riffraff of holy myriad flower petals
Like flamethrowers made into grace notes.
Your sentence is filigree, hammered metal

Beautiful enough to be the skin of light.
Only because of you, is heaven in sight.

Go Ahead, Be Glum

But we're having none of it. The children
Have set a mountain range in our reason,

Wrapped a rainbow around the house. They
Hold hands, a mountain lion comes to them
Golden-eyed, to lick their faces. She will stay

With them forever. She will defend them
Forever. As they play, inside the house,
Nothing special: they give dolls a dose
Of poetry, while in the stove the bread

Gathers from centuries a savory gold
Just to make a crust. And what gem
Is this, crisscrossed with light, in the fold

Of a kitchen towel? It is common treasure—
Love's mischief, without limit or measure.

Plain Offering to the Materialist

What is it to heal? By what you give,
By old summertime in your touch, live

In trust. We say that flesh is a trace
Of dust, yet daring, since even light
Is just beginning work. Each grace,

After all, is refined of raw soul. You
Must do this work; all musicks await
Within you, to arise when you do
What the falcons say. A path straight

From morning leads onward to where
You will answer that radiance. Sight
Is the template of soul-travel. Care

Is both rough sense and lucent movement.
Freedom is your going where you are sent.

The Coast of Maine

Even shadows delicious—soft, expectant,
Like a woman ready for bed. A content

Of soul is here, amused, resurgent in peace.
Tides feather-step with the moon. A heron
Cries out, her phrase a line, then a crease,

Then the crack in the air: and we see
Into the centermost of world, a story
Within our story, joke in death, a glory
That is source of all earthly life—tree,

Waterfall, joke, idea, wedding, revelation—
What is permanent, clownish secret, boon
And bounty and raucous gift, waystation

Of daily life open everywhere to the union
And study that is loving, that is communion.

Moments in the Life of a Common Man

Floral delicious cut-loose pleasures of the one
I love; a wild river, showing just where the sun

With its flammable grace notes comes through
Big cedars standing along the blessed canyon;
A mystery of things, written in azure and true

Script on oceans at twilight. A ramshackle house
Where people cook together, tasting and talking,
Seasoning the hour with laughter. Our walking
Into the high desert to mark out a course

Of souls through coyote, sagebrush, magpie
And cottonwood: all the world we see begun
Again, made for peace, where we may die

Into the open secret: earth undefiled
And sunlight in the voice of every child.

The ABC of Understanding

Some days you do less so
You can love more; and so

Because of loving you follow flights
Of cranes across the sky, and you can
Deliver honey hidden in morning light

To the hands of a child who then can heal
Friend and strangers of a first suffering—
Birthmark of earth. A grace and turning
Of the world to hidden cadence, the seal

Of unrecognized design on a letter sent
From the next world, at last you can
Understand. Mastery is perfect obedience.

Heart is a skylight. Soul can make a wish.
In secret, you must learn how to vanish.

The Bees of the Invisible

It means something, that you are nothing.
Darkness thickens, men go scuffling—

Venomous teeth fastened on centuries:
Marked as somebody, they came to carve
Their initials in history, who then buries

All of them. The soil will cure them
Of the swagger. Now become nothing,
You will cure history of them, you
Are ready for this easygoing light, when

Secret heaven comes again to search
For song-led eyes and sovereign heart
Await within us, body's hidden torch

Ready to work again, luminous, alive—
When you are the honey in the hive.

Genesis, Revised

Across water a canter of light, drumbeat
Of beauty's music on shore. Lovers meet

Close by, rough in bed: their hands have
The salt of reality. They answer pleasure
The way water answers wind, they have

Single movement, lucid sweat, summer
Improvisation and curiosity. They meant
To give all they are given; they meant
To dazzle by their vanishing. They endure

By loss; the songline within such love
Makes simple fact beyond measure:
They would see old paradise above

Become young heaven on earth. On earth.
Life begins here. This morning is the first.

Once More Day in the Great Basin

The air a classroom, dust a teacher;
Lawful sailing mustang, our leader

In passage from world and world, as
Dustdevils whirl and reminisce, ravens
Draw a double moondog, saints pass

To talk with bull snakes in the grass;
Antelope bolt, by their jokes and grace
Open up a stone canyon, they race
Morning to a golden mesa, then at last

Meet to make together the stillness of noon.
We hear dialogue of coyotes in their dens,
They climb the sky to the crescent moon,

Then visit us tonight with bemused power,
Singing the music of the meteor shower.

This Means You

As a solar flare arcs through darkness, as
Tropical night is the future of music, as

Parrots fly into the next world to bring
Us laughter and scintillation, wildflowers
Are found in a forest on the moon: sing

To have such ordinary work. Sing: since
Earth is ragamuffin of heaven, so must
You cartwheel in air with ravens, must
Call bobcats inside your house, since

Time is bedecked with chance, now
You live and die, your mildest powers
Turn a cyclone into a raindrop. Now,

Beloved. Delay is suicide. To survive
On a jetstream of soul, ride, and ride.

Once Again—Have I Got This Right?

Say, then, there is more than hunger.
Beyond brain's lightning and thunder

Comes a clear life-giving spring rain
Of understanding, when what you see
Will marry at last what you do. Pain

And joy, life and death, pinwheel galaxy
And sand-grain, meet and touch in a bar
And go home together. What they know
Is how heat is hope and earth is a star;

And what they make is life. And then
There is more than suffering, than beauty,
There are worlds and worlds to defend,

A phrase touches off dynamite of meaning—
Sacred light within light, world-revealing.

One Day, You Knew ...

How centerpoint of paradise, is the star
Within your head, beyond the pulse; star

In your palm as you reach for the face
Of the one you love. So the blessing
Comes like a gust of ancestral grace,

Time is tossed aside, space gathers
A tempest of peaceable beauties, gathers
You and islands and hummingbirds, gathers
Sage, rubies, darkness, the blues; gathers

Dust and derring-do of children: everything
That has been loved, comes forth, pressing
Forward to construct your particolored wing,

A future and final, first life: you
Are more than angels. You. You.

Awakening After a Night of Snow

Crescendo of delicacy, original crystal, fall
Together into a dancehall of softness, call

Through cold of white sailing unsurmountable
Curious travelers, hum of bemused storytellers
Who fold their light within, waiting, uncountable

In old secret glistening, which they show
When sunlight answers them; ambassadors
Of symmetry, whose skyborn idea restores
Our faith in order and our hope to know

All a generosity in playfulness; our couriers
Of clarity, as if they visited from interstellar
Space, to touch with blessing the worriers,

The sorrowful, the hapless, the lost, the dead:
The deliverance, in darkness, of what light said.

Theory of Evolution

It is the way evolution works: lightning
In the mind marries the way you sing

To movement in earth of molten diamond;
Marries the rhythm of spiced trade winds
To lovemaking by the fire in a cabin sunk

Among snowdrifts; marries what a woman
Whispers to the child in her arms, to a gust
Of wind lustrous upon the ocean. This trust
By mind of heart, cherished reader, when

You were born, was within you: was you:
You connected worlds, on you depends
Every day the unity of life, what is true

Beyond illusion, pain, assumption, fraud.
You are thunderbolt, dirt, maggot, god.

A Helpful Hidden Man

He loved candles because he thought
His life was like that flame, thought

His light was just that fragile. He
Trusted the world the way the flame
Of a candle trusts the wind. So he

Shone, pointed to the heavens. He
Loved, because he burned and burned
Himself. Himself only. He returned
Every radiance. All that he was, he

Burned. And he knew, even as was lit
The light of homecoming, that his brain
Held stars and peacocks, dust, twilit

Original ocean, parrot, song, death.
For his own flame he drew a breath.

The Small, the Daily, the Ordinary

It's just lichen on a rock. It means
That a mountain will fall, its seams

A songbook of dust and gravel. It's just
Honey on the tongue of a daughter, it means
That one day in the tropics she will trust

Thick sweet light on a man she desires.
It's just the deep-sea rambling of currents,
Mysterious journeywork, giving assurance
To a young woman whose mind has fires

That need a cooling ocean, else they
Consume her. It's just ancient streams
Of starlight in our galaxy: as you pray

In wild country you know your last breath
Will call a cascade of light into your death.

He Died

He thought: so flesh is clothes. So
We go there with only what we know,

And we know just what we love,
Nothing more. Despite the pain, now
He can forge memory anew: a sieve

That lets drain darkness only, so that
He came to know a concentrate of light.
In death then he threw off all of night,
Unfastening a fleshly cloak. On a rack

Of ignorance he had lived, so many years.
Whence comes, then, the laughter? How
Did death offer such comedy? The tears

At the pain were path for lightning. The science
Of dying is delectation, surety, phosphorescence.

All the Music I Have

As fate wraps me in a freezing cloak,
Time stalks and strangles as I choke,

Stars and oceans vanish, golden eagles
Fly to a bounty of light now streaming
Away from me; as diabolical cold pulls

My heart under a black hammer of silence,
All music ripped from my tissue, my hours
Ransacked, pulverized, the world's flowers
Gone off to grace and conjuration, my license

To live now cancelled by some final power
Of famished soil: as a tempestuous seeming
In my life crushes me in shame, my sour

Failures set off depth charges, I will call
In thankfulness, thankfulness, as I fall.

When

When from a poem comes a golden eagle,
When the klaxon horns of hatred go still,

When a gray wolf and Plato sit down
In the kitchen and play chess; when stones
Move at night in a canyon, and resound

With homely music, so that we see across
The night sky a raucous current of colors
In concord with new stars; when brothers
And sisters, the hurt, the hungry, the lost,

Children everywhere taste honey through;
When a pulse of light at the center of bone
Draws from you a song, and in love, you

Stand there alone in the desert to sing:
When you and world together take wing—

Where God Went

To have coffee. To do a cartwheel
In soft grass in the morning. To kneel

And give thanks to have given to us
A chance to give thanks. To throw back
Whiskey in a rough bar in the wilderness.

To be a young woman, dancing. To be
An old woman, singing Verdi in a church
On a hilltop in Italy. To set forever free
Gentleness in a man. With a hand on earth

To trace Arctic storms and trade winds.
To hold a baby, read a book; to track
With praise and adoration giant fins

Of whales in migration. To paint oceans blue.
To remember. God went to see you.

Why Do Such Ordinary Work?

It's because we know a pen on paper
May be the axis of a planet; or a saber

Hung on the belt of a woman who walks
Across the clouds; may be a finger
Touching a tambourine to music a fox

Will come to hear. A pen on the page
Moves like a cat on rooftops, a gazelle
Through a canyon, an actress on a stage
Who as she speaks will cast a spell

With letters of light, in words we need
That come after language, to assure
Whatever we say is so much seed,

Soon to be planted in the furrow left
By a pen plowing paper—in that cleft.

Remembering Life on Earth

Order within, makes the order without.
In a countryside of soul, you walk about.

A spark in the mind is solar flare.
What you dream is what you dare.
An idea at midnight is a world's fair.

A tapping foot is music of the spheres.
Memory of a lover melts all a century.
A hand of death brushes off all fears.
Story in her eyes is song and treasury.

A way you love beckons every beauty.
One cartwheel turns dust into a mare.
A promise kept, stars report for duty.

Our children know what heavens need.
Cosmos is soil. Earth is a seed.

Quick Notes on the Reader and Her Labors

In the wall of tiles, a network of worlds.
In the phrase of a woman, handful of pearls.

Color of dawn in the tropics, is her skin
At the midmost of pleasure. In snowflakes
Of the blizzard, birth of galaxies. The spin

And somersault of a child bears grace
So irresistible, it will stop the wheel
Of fortune, clear out history, make a deal
With time, so that then her honest face

Holds all peaceable rambunctious beauty.
In a gust of wind, a blessed force shakes
Free the jewels of the soul. We will see

Them traded for liberty, for life, for a dream
Made real by the music of what you mean.

She Works, and This is Her Name

True, we are material, yet mated
With dream. Random chemistry, fated

To be in just this place, this time.
Decomposing every day, yet making
Amorous transcendental dance, or a rhyme

In a dark room on a cold night, a painting
In a cheap attic in a big city; or giving
Everything you have, today, before giving
Everything again tomorrow, never waiting

And unknown to everyone. Love is
Anonymous. God is anonymous. Creating
The world, is continuous, and it is

Just the way you live, plain and free.
Brash dirt, nothing, sacred: a beauty.

Water

Candor made material, origin of grace;
At a mountain spring, unmistakable taste

Of a promise kept; clarity on the loose
And on the lookout for love, seeking always
A level with heaven; our caterwauling truth

In waterfalls and long rapids, storm waves
And floodtides that bear the flaring silks
Of sunrise; young beautiful mother's milk
Of all life; in our sorrow, what saves

Us, with demonstration of eddies, pirouettes,
Whirlpools, coral reef and rainbow, cays,
A lovemaking rhythm in tides that accepts

Us into a sensuality and religion of the sea:
A poem is made of water, of you, and of me.

Coming Home to Sonnets

After such traveling, I would return home
To sonnets written in the center of bone

And brain; in them, script of ocean currents,
Rising of newly molten rock, a sparkling
In the hands of a child whose opalescence

Is a sign of prophetic arts; to sonnets
Having the cadence of a coyote's walk,
Music of a barn dance, or celestial talk
Of two angels in a tavern making bets

On when heaven would come through the door
With storytelling beauty, a beggar and king
By her side. The world is what we will pour

For her to drink. By the fire she'll stand,
Planets in her eyes, and a sonnet in hand.

COLOPHON

Designed and produced by Bob Blesse at the Black Rock Press, University of Nevada, Reno. The typeface is Dante, designed by Giovanni Mardersteig. The display font is Rialto, designed by Giovanni de Faccio and Lui Karner in Austria. Printed and bound by Thomson-Shore, Inc., Dexter, Michigan.